# Creative W

*Amanda J Harrington*

Creative Writing for Kids vol 1

# Contents

4

# Introduction

All too often, children are put off creative writing by feeling they have to do it *right*. I want to help children enjoy writing their own stories. Creativity comes in lots of different packages, and not just the ones marked with a red tick or a gold star!

This book comes from original exercises and activities created especially for one-to-one lessons, creative writing groups, school visits and for my own children when they were home educated. The focus is on fun and creative thinking, so that literacy and writing skills happen more naturally without it feeling like work.

The age range for all the books in the Creative Writing for Kids range is 7-14, depending on ability. Lots of exercises can be expanded to suit keen writers and many have been written for reluctant learners and special needs students.

# How to Use this Book

When working through the book, children should only be thinking about their stories or poems. I have deliberately left out any mention of spelling, punctuation, grammar and other technical matters. This book is about enjoying creativity and freeing children so that they are not afraid to try new things and attempt more challenging work.

The exercises are for a variety of ages and abilities, but can all be adapted to suit individual children. I have known children who could barely write who created wonderful stories through pictures and conversations, using these exercises. Confident writers can adapt the work to suit themselves and expand from it as much as they like.

The exercises can be completed in any order and there are linked themes, such as free story-telling or poetry, throughout the book.

# Draw and Write: Favourite Place

Draw a picture of your favourite place. This can be somewhere you like to go, or a place you have never been but would love to visit.

Now describe the place in words, using the picture to help you. Imagine you have to answer questions about it, as if you are describing it to someone who has never been there before.

Look at the next page for some ideas to help you.

## Think about:

1. Where is it?

2. What kind of place is it?

3. Who goes there with you?

4. Why do you like it so much?

## Example

*My favourite place is the farm because I can help with the animals and play with my Gran's dog, Caspar. The farm is big, with lots of fields and has sheep and 2 horses.*

# A Story in Pictures: The Scary Path

You are going to make a story, using only pictures. In this story, you are walking along a path and you are afraid.

Using pictures drawn by yourself, cut from a book or printed from a computer, show your journey along the scary path.

You can add titles, but otherwise your pictures must tell the story.

# Jumble Words: Mrs Fickle

Mrs Fickle has opened a new shop. So far, we know nothing about Mrs Fickle or her shop.

Look at the words below. Choose **at least 3** from each list, then write a short story describing Mrs Fickle and her shop.

You can also draw pictures, using the words you have chosen to help you.

**Mrs Fickle**

*Jolly, clever, tall, fat, freckle, hat, stern, giggles, grey, ginger, red, old, loud, friendly, cold, young, pretty, cat, curly, fussy, sleepy.*

**Her Shop**

*Small, smelly, sweets, flowers, counter, soap, vegetables, fresh, paintings, big, empty, books, paper, toys, games, clothes, food.*

# Tell the Tale: Away We Go!

Look at the picture and think of a story to match it. If you have an idea, just try to write about it.

If you need some extra help:

*1. How do you think the girl is feeling?*

*2. Where do you think she is going?*

*3. How did she learn how to fly?*

# Story Practice: A Beary Short Tail

You are a brown bear called Fudge and you live in a cave on the edge of the forest. One day, you catch a hunter and use a People spell. Instantly, you have swapped places with the hunter.

You look like a man but inside you're still a bear. You tie up the hunter at the back of the cave and set off for town.

Now write about what happens when you get there.

# Comic Strip: Otto Loves TV

Make a story in a comic strip. You can make it as long or as short as you like, but there are three things you need to know to help you:

1. Otto loves TV!

2. Otto loves swimming.

3. Otto likes experimenting.

# Freestyle: Good Times

Here are some ideas for you to use in a story or a poem. Make your story or poem as long or as short as you like.

You can decide what happens in it and who your characters are.

Just choose one of the ideas and have a go.

1. A tree covered in lights.

2. A trip to the beach.

3. A table full of chocolate eggs.

4. A candle-lit pumpkin.

5. A present with your name on it.

6. Going on holiday.

7. A giant jar full of pennies.

8. Having a party.

9. Getting a little brother or sister.

10. A water slide on a hot day.

# Double Act: Runn~ing

You are going to write a story, but there are two things you need to include in it.

One is that there must be lots of **movement** in the story.

The other is that at least 7 words must end in the **'ing'** sound. Have a go!

# Tell the Tale: Peeking!

What kind of a story goes with this picture? It can be any kind of story you like, but think about:

*1. How is the boy feeling?*

*2. Is he playing a game or really hiding?*

*3. Where is he hiding?*

# Adventures into the Unknown:

# The Climb

Write a poem, using the three ideas below. You decide how long your poem should be and whether or not you want it to rhyme.

1. You are climbing over very hard ground

2. You almost fall.

3. You hear strange noises.

*Remember!*

*A poem does not have to rhyme or be very long. Just have a go!*

# Freestyle: Scary Stuff

Here are some ideas for you to use in a story or a poem. Make your story or poem as long or as short as you like.

You can decide what happens in it and who your characters are.

Just choose one of the ideas and have a go.

1. A dark room.

2. Homework.

3. A spider's web in the corner.

4. A wasp's nest.

5. Educational television.

6. Falling out with your friends.

7. The Ghost Train.

8. Meeting new people.

9. A noise in the night.

10. Getting lost.

# Jumble Words: Characters

Look at the words below. Choose some of them to create **two different people.**

For instance, you could choose 'Miss' and 'Egg' to create 'Miss Egg' as one of your characters.

*Simon Lock Pippa Miss Jilly Anna Benjamin Jumbles Mr*

*Anthony Clover Mrs Penny Emma Carter Buttons Winter*

*Mortimer Pennyworth Bud Alfred Doctor Gray Harvest Jake*

## *What are they like?*

Write down the names of your two characters. Now answer these questions about them:

1. What colour hair do they have?

2. Are they friendly?

3. What is their favourite food?

4. Are they young or old?

5. Do they have a pet?

6. Do they live on their own?

Now you can draw pictures of your characters, to match your description.

After you have created your character, think of what kind of story you might see them in. You can either write the story, or describe what might happen in the story.

# Story Words: Mixture

Look at the headings below and think of as many words as you can to go with each one. I have given you some words to get you started.

Then choose at least **two** words from each heading and put them into a story. You decide how long you want the story to be. Look at the examples to help you.

Colours: *red*

Weather: *sunny*

Animals: *leopard*

Feelings: *grumpy*

*Example story (very short!): The grumpy leopard sat on the red sand, resting in the sunshine.*

# Story Practice: Princess Angelica

Angelica has always been the worst princess in the palace. One day she finds a spinning wheel in the attic and pricks her finger, hoping Prince Charming will come.

Instead, she opens the door and finds herself on the top floor of a modern shopping centre. She can go back, prick her finger and return to her own land, or carry on into this new world. What happens next?

# Double Act: Sudden-ly

You are going to write a story, but there are two things you need to include in it.

One is that there must be a **surprise.**

The other is that at least 5 words in your story must end in the **'ly'** sound. Have a go!

# Poster Perfect: Wanted!

Draw a picture of yourself or find a photo and stick it onto a piece of paper.

Next, imagine you are making a Wanted poster for a terrible villain - *you* are the villain!

There are two important things you need to include on your poster: the **crime** you committed and the **reward** for your capture. Everything else is up to you!

# Comic Strip: Jenny's Foot

This story is going to be a comic strip, with a set of pictures and words to tell the story.

You don't need many words when you are using pictures, just a few to explain what is happening and speech bubbles if you want to show people talking.

Look at the sentences on the next page. They are in the wrong order. You need to rearrange them and then make a comic strip story around them.

## *Sentences*

Her foot was twice as big as it should be.

Jenny's mother hated snails.

The shoes looked beautiful!

Jenny's friend, Claire, had very big feet.

She tiptoed across the garden.

"Oh no!" she cried.

Jenny loved shoes.

She had to hop all the way to the bathroom.

Claire loved football.

The snails didn't care

It was everywhere!

# Adventures into the Unknown: The New Start

Write a poem, using the three ideas below. You decide how long your poem should be and whether or not you want it to rhyme.

If you like, you can write it as a tiny story, then turn it into a poem.

1. You have to go somewhere for the first time.

2. Everyone else seems happy.

3. Memories of how things used to be.

# Tell the Tale: In the Snow!

Think of a story to go with this picture about being in the snow.

It can be any kind of story you like, as long as it matches the picture in some way.

## *Think about:*

*1. Some people love snow and some people hate it.*

*2. There is fake snow as well as the real thing!*

*3. You might have to travel to find proper snow.*

# Story Recipe: Your Story

You are the main character in this story, so write it in the **first person.** This means writing things like, 'I did' or 'I want to' and 'I felt' etc. The story can be as long or as short as you like.

As well as having **yourself** in the story, you need to include:

*Next door's cat*

*A new friend*

*A hundred newspapers*

# Write a Letter: You're Famous!

You've been asked to write to your fans, telling them how you became famous and what your life is like.

Decide what you want to be famous for. Will you be a pop star, footballer, writer or something else?

Then write your letter, with as many details as possible about your life and what it is like to be you.

# Adventures into the Unknown: The Puppy

Write a poem, using the three ideas below. You decide how long your poem should be and whether or not you want it to rhyme.

1. A really bad smell.

2. A half-eaten shoe.

3. Nibbles.

# Story Practice: Mrs Wrinklebottom

Mrs Wrinklebottom is your neighbour and she hates you. She thinks you make too much noise and run about a lot, even if you sit quietly and say nothing! Mrs Wrinklebottom is a big, scary woman so you are too frightened to make friends with her.

One day, your mother sends you round with some cakes for Mrs Wrinklebottom. You sneak in and leave them on the kitchen table. On your way out, you see Mrs Wrinklebottom in her hall cupboard. She hasn't seen you. A mad moment takes you over and you shut the cupboard door and lock it. Just for a second you enjoy it, then she starts to hammer on the door.

"Let me out!" she booms. "I know who did this! Wait till your mother finds out!"

Now you daren't let her out. It's too scary to think what she might do if you open the door, but you can't leave her in there forever. What should you do?

# Draw and Write: Look Around You

Draw a picture of what you see around you, right now. Put as much detail into it as you can.

Now describe what is around you in words.

## *Think about*

What is near you?

Are there any people?

What do you like about where you are?

Where would you rather be?

# Freestyle: Moving Around

Here are some ideas for you to use in a story or a poem. Make your story or poem as long or as short as you like.

You can decide what happens in it and who your characters are.

Just choose one of the ideas and have a go.

## *Ideas*

1. A short journey.

2. When we moved house.

3. A broken down car.

4. A cat running across a meadow.

5. The wheelie bin rolling off down the street.

6. Smoke from a bonfire curling up into the sky.

7. An ant scurrying across a picnic cloth.

8. Getting onto an aeroplane.

9. A rowing boat.

10. When Jessica's bag fell out of the bus.

# Story Recipe: A Day Out

You are the main character in this story, so write it in the **first person.** This means writing things like, 'I did' or 'I want to' and 'I felt' etc.

As well as having yourself in the story, you need to include:

*An unexpected stop*

*A half-sucked sweet*

*A grass covered hill*

*A loud voice*

# Story Practice: The Magic Pocket

## *Part One*

You are given a pair of jeans for your birthday. Every time you put your hand in your pocket, you find a ten pound note. The pocket is magical and will refill with money each time you empty it. What do you do?

You can draw pictures to tell your story as well as writing.

## *Part Two*

It is Saturday morning. You wake up late, ready to have more fun with the money coming out of your magic pocket. That's when you realise your jeans have been put in the wash.

When they're dry, you put them on and look in the pocket. You find a very small potato. What happens next? Does the magic pocket still work? Or does it only make potatoes now?

Write the rest of the story or tell it in pictures.

# Tell the Tale: Popping!

Think of the word 'popping' and write a story to go with it and this picture.

## *Think about:*

*1. Some people don't like balloons.*

*2. Does a party need to have balloons?*

*3. How does the little girl in the picture feel?*

# Draw and Write: Where I live

Draw a picture of your home. Now describe your home in words, using your picture to help you.

## *Think about:*

*Do you live in a house or a bungalow?*

*A boat or a castle?*

*In a caravan or a flat?*

*What colour is your front door?*

*Do you have a garden?*

# Double Act: Decorat~ed

You are going to write a story, but there are two things you need to include in it.

One is that your story must be about the **Christmas** season.

The other is that at least 7 words must end in the **'ed'** sound. Have a go!

# Adventures into the Unknown: The Visit

Write a poem, using the three ideas below. You decide how long your poem should be and whether or not you want it to rhyme.

1. You have to visit someone.

2. You feel afraid.

3. You are surprised.

# Story Practice: Professor Nibbles

Every time you pass the hutch, you hear strange noises but when you open the door you only see Nibbles the guinea pig, eating food.

One day, you decide to find out what is going on. Creeping quietly up to the hutch, you slowly open the door. Inside, Nibbles is hammering at some kind of machine that takes up most of the room.

Suddenly, Nibbles spots you. He pats the side of the hutch and the wood slides right round, taking the machine away into a hidden room. Even when you look behind the hutch you can't see where it has gone.

What happens next?

# Write a Letter: Saying Sorry

You need to write a letter to someone, saying you're sorry.

You can decide what you have done and who you are apologising to.

You can also decide whether it is a good apology, or if you don't really mean it and only want to get out of trouble!

Don't forget to include details of what you did wrong.

# Double Act: Swimm~er!

You are going to write a story, but there are two things you need to include in it.

One is that there must be **sporty** things in your story.

The other is that you should have at least 6 words ending in the **'er'** sound. Have a go!

# A Story in Pictures: A Royal Baby

You are going to make a story, using only pictures. In this story, a new prince or princess has been born into a magical kingdom.

Using pictures drawn by yourself, cut from a book or printed from a computer, tell the story of the new baby. You can add titles, but otherwise your pictures must tell the story.

Don't forget to use lots of shiny colours in this story, as a royal baby will be given presents of gold, silver and jewels.

# Tell the Tale! Water Slide

Think of a water slide and write a story to go with it.

It can be any kind of story you like, as long as it includes the water slide.

Don't forget, it doesn't have to be a big slide in a pool; it could be a slide in your back garden, with a hose pipe running down it.

# Story Practice: The Lizard

Your friend Klaus is going on holiday and he wants you to look after his pet lizard, Boris. The trouble is, your parents *never* let you have any pets in the house.

You end up sneaking Boris the lizard into the house in your sports bag. He seems quite happy in there, so you leave him in the bag until everyone has gone to bed.

In the darkened house you open the bag to take Boris out. But he isn't there!

You search your room and then try to search the rest of the house but there's no sign of Boris. What happens next?

# Story Recipe: Gnomes, Bats and a Ring

You are the main character in this story, so write it in the **first person.** This means writing things like, 'I did' or 'I want to' and 'I felt' etc.

As well as having yourself in the story, you need to include:

*a garden gnome coming to life*

*bats in the night*

*a diamond ring sparkling in the darkness*

# Poster Perfect: Guinea Pigs Galore!

Your guinea pigs have had babies. And the babies have had babies. It's reached the stage where you either need to find them new homes or move out and they can have the house to themselves.

Design a poster to advertise your guinea pigs. Make them sound as beautiful and friendly as you can, and include lots of pictures so that people will want to buy them.

Try not to tell any lies about your guinea pigs but do your best to make people want to give them homes.

# Story Practice: Furry Trousers

You bring your pet rat, Archie, into school one day so you can show him to your friends.

Unfortunately, Archie escapes from your bag and and runs into the school kitchen. He eats some lovely, juicy, mysteriously sparkly berries in a golden basket. Once he's eaten them all, he comes back to find you.

As soon as you touch him, you start to grow fur. Nice, soft, grey fur, like Archie's. Before you know it, you're covered in fur and can only squeak. You look down at Archie, to see if he's okay.

'Gosh! This is exciting!' he says, grinning up at you.

What happens next?

# Tell the tale: Topsy-turvy!

Oh dear! Everything seems to have been turned upside down. Or is it you that is the wrong way up?

Write a story based on this picture. You can make it about yourself or someone else.

## *Think about:*

*1. How did this happen?*

*2. Is it exciting or scary?*

57

*3. What could you do if you could walk on ceilings and up walls?*

*4. What happens if you can't control it?*

*5. And what could go wrong?*

# Story Recipe: Mysteries

You are the main character in this story, so write it in the **first person.** This means writing things like, 'I did' or 'I want to' and 'I felt' etc.

As well as having yourself in the story, you need to include:

*A locked cupboard*

*An open book*

*A hidden secret*

# Adventures into the Unknown: The Boat Trip

Write a poem, using the three ideas below. You decide how long your poem should be and whether or not you want it to rhyme.

1. Life jackets.

2. A gust of wind.

3. The mist whispering around your face.

# Tell the Tale: Merry Christmas!

Write a story about this little girl and her Christmas. Will something exciting happen?

## *Think about:*

*1. How does the little girl feel?*

*2. Is she having a good day?*

*3. Do you think she got what she wanted for Christmas?*

# Poster Perfect: Any Old Thing

You need to make some money, and fast, but the only thing you have to sell is an old coat. It has holes in the pockets and two buttons left. There is a hole in the back too.

Make a poster to sell the old coat. You can draw pictures, cut some out from books or print them out from a computer. The main thing is, you must make this poor old coat seem so **wonderful** that people can't resist it.

See what you can think of to make it seem fabulous!

Don't forget to describe the coat and tell people how much it costs.

# Double Act: Butter-y

You are going to write a story, but there are two things you need to include in it.

One is that there must be **food** in your story.

The other is that at least 5 words must end in the '**y**' sound. Have a go!

# Tell the Tale: I'm not going to!

Write a story about this picture, including as many describing words as you can.

## *Think about:*

*1. What time of year is it?*

*2. Do you think the little girl is grumpy or enjoying herself?*

*3. What do you think happened to make her pull a face?*

# A Story in Pictures: A Little Visitor

You are going to make a story, using only pictures. In this story, your little cousin Derek has come to visit. He is only two and loves to run around, playing with things. He often breaks what he plays with.

Using pictures drawn by yourself, cut from a book or printed from a computer, tell the story of his visit. You can add titles, but otherwise your pictures must tell the story.

# Write a Letter: A New Pen Pal

You are writing to someone who lives far away from you. This is the first letter you have ever sent them, so you need to tell them all about yourself.

Include what you like to do, where you live and anything else you think they need to know.

Don't forget to ask them about themselves. If you are going to be pen pals, you need to be interested in their life too.

# Story Recipe: Four Legs and Feelings

You are the main character in this story, so write it in the **first person**. This means writing things like, 'I did' or 'I want to' and 'I felt' etc.

As well as having yourself in the story, you need to include:

*a friendly goat*

*an angry sheep*

*a greedy little dog*

# Story Practice: A Woolly Jumper

Auntie Peggy has spent weeks knitting you a lovely new jumper. She knows you like colourful things so she used every spare ball of wool she had and mixed them together. Secretly, you hate your new jumper because it makes you look like a giant sweet but you promise to wear it every time Auntie Peggy visits.

Today Auntie Peggy is coming for lunch. You put on the jumper and take your dog for a walk. Then you wriggle under your bed looking for a game you lost. After that, you play chase with the dog in your garden.

As Auntie Peggy arrives, you look out at the back garden. There is something trailing all over the grass, and on the trees. It's something multi-coloured…

With a sinking heart, you look down at your jumper and see it is only half there. The other half is tangled round everything in the back garden. Even the dog has a bright woolly tail!

With only seconds to spare before Auntie Peggy walks in, what will you do?

# Double Act: Happi-ness

You are going to write a story, but there are two things you need to include in it.

One is that there must be a lot of **feelings** in your story (you can choose more than one emotion).

The other is that at least 4 words must end in the **'ness'** sound. Have a go!

# Tell the Tale: I don't know!

Look at this picture of a boy surrounded by sums and puzzles.
Write a story about him and what is happening in the picture.

## *Think about:*

*1. Is he happy?*

*2. What do you think will happen next?*

*3. Would you like to be the boy?*

# Story Recipe: Time Out

You are the main character in this story, so write it in the **first person.** This means writing things like, 'I did' or 'I want to' and 'I felt' etc.

As well as having yourself in the story, you need to include:

*your favourite game*

*TV on loud*

*playing on the beach*

*relaxing in your room*

# A Story in Pictures: The Holiday

You are going to make a story, using only pictures. In this story, you are going on holiday.

Using pictures drawn by yourself, cut from a book or printed from a computer, tell the story of your holiday. You can add titles, but otherwise your pictures must tell the story.

You can tell the story of a real holiday you have been on, or you can make up an imaginary holiday, where anything can happen.

# Jumble Words: Diary of a Bad Week

You are filling in your diary. Look at the jumbled sentences and decide which day of the week they should be.

You can also draw pictures to decorate your week.

**Days: Sunday Monday Tuesday Wednesday Thursday Friday Saturday**

1. The handle fell off the bathroom door and I was stuck in there for an hour. I was late for school.

2. My cat was sick on my homework but the teacher thought it was me.

3. My little brother thinks worms are great and when I got home from school he had made them a home in my moneybox.

4. My mother wants us to eat healthy food. This is the third day I've had pineapple chunks in my lunch box.

5. The TV broke and I had to spend the morning doing my homework.

6. I was ill after eating too many pineapple chunks and had to stay

off school. Brilliant!

7. I opened my school bag in the middle of class and found my little brother had put the cat in there again. It took three teachers and a dinner lady to catch it.

# Freestyle: Good Little Things

Here are some ideas for you to use in a story or a poem. Make your story or poem as long or as short as you like.

You can decide what happens in it and who your characters are.

Just choose one of the ideas and have a go.

1. A sledge on the snow.

2. Birthday cards with money in them.

3. A new packet of sweets.

4. A holiday full of sunshine.

5. Knowing how to work a DVD player.

6. My dog can answer the phone.

7. Breakfast in bed.

8. A trip to the toy shop.

9. My cat can catch spiders.

10. Glow-in-the-dark moon and stars.

# Tell the Tale: Cabbages!

That is a very big cabbage! Write a story about the little girl and the giant cabbage.

## *Think about:*

*1. Is it a real cabbage?*

*2. How did she get there?*

*3. Does she like cabbages?*

# Story Recipe: Loved Things

You are the main character in this story, so write it in the **first person.** This means writing things like, 'I did' or 'I want to' and 'I felt' etc.

As well as having yourself in the story, you need to include:

*a well-loved book*

*a golden key*

*a favourite thing*

# Draw and Write: Your Birthday

Draw a picture of your best birthday. This could be a picture of the presents, or the party, or even of you, enjoying yourself!

Now describe the birthday in words, using the picture to help you.

What made this birthday the best one? Was it the presents or the people around you?

What would your best present be, if you could have anything in the world?

# Adventures into the Unknown: The Phone Box

Write a poem, using the three ideas below. You decide how long your poem should be and whether or not you want it to rhyme.

*A lit phone box*

*An unexpected call*

*A new adventure*

# Story Recipe: The New Doll

You are the main character in this story, so write it in the **first person.** This means writing things like, 'I did' or 'I want to' and 'I felt' etc.

As well as having yourself in the story, you need to include:

*A new doll*

*A sound in the corner*

*A little footstep*

# Freestyle: I'm a Hero!

Here are some ideas for you to use in a story or a poem. Make your story or poem as long or as short as you like.

You can decide what happens in it and who your characters are.

Just choose one of the ideas and have a go.

*1.A great disguise*

*2. Jumping very high*

*3. A trusty sidekick*

*4. A quick-thinking friend*

5. *A magical item*

6. *Super strength*

7. *Where did she go?*

8. *A grand plan to take over the world*

9. *A shining cape.*

10. *I'm the hero!*

Ready for more?

If you would like more creative writing ideas, visit www.amandajharrington.co.uk or http://freebrians.blogspot.co.uk for news of creative writing courses and free resources.

You might also like:

Printed in Great Britain
by Amazon